Cont

FOOTBALL CRAZY

Football Philosophy

If the world is a football
spinning round in space
then, who was it who
kicked it there
in the first place?

Andrew Collett

Football Rules OK

Football

Football
is to share.
A game
for everyone
everywhere.

Football
should be clean.
Fulfilment
of the plain
man's dream.

Football
should be true.
To loyal
fans like me.
Like you.

Ann Bonner

Football For Beginners

OK,
It's very simple.
All you have to do is
kick or head this leather
thing to their end of the
pitch (don't touch it
with your hand),
then

get it

Make sure it's underneath this bar (there's a net behind it) and

just right of this bit of wood.

also to the left of this post.

Got it?

Charles Thomson

Rules of the Game

Our school has no field so we can only play
football in the yard—and it's small, so Thursday
is when we're allowed to bring in our balls—
and that's the first rule. I've noticed that all
games need rules, and in each game there are some
you can't play without—like if you throw one
when you play snakes and ladders, that's how far
you must move, but you could agree to start
at the top and go down ladders and up the snakes
and still have a good game. So it doesn't make
much difference to us if there's five on one
side and six on the other, or if we all run
together after the ball and don't have a goalie—
you understand—rules are just what you agree
among yourselves—over the wire fence is definitely
off the pitch and getting in the big boys' way
is asking for trouble. Being rude to the janitor
will get you sent inside and kicking spectators
or their lunch-boxes is not allowed—
you have to tolerate the crowd
and you might start a fight that stops the game.
Most of the simple rules we keep the same,
no hands, no fists, no deliberate tripping,
no pulling shirts until they tear, no sitting
on the ball unless you're really in goal.

11

That's about it. But playing after the bell's gone
could mean suspension. And you'd be a total nitwit
to pick up the ball and run away with it.
That's not playing the same game any more.
That's rugby, or a declaration of war.

Dave Calder

Boys' Game?

'This is our side of the playground,
What are you doing here?
You want to play football?
That's a laugh!
It's a boys' game. Got it clear?'

'Actually, Kev, she's pretty good,
Especially in goal.
I saw her down the rec last night:
She was really in control.
Saved a penalty early on,
And from corners . . . can't she catch!

Dived several times
At their striker's feet—
Really kept us in the match.'

'Well, in that case . . .
Of course, it's actually
In goal where we're really weak.
I mean, anyone's got to be better
Than Baggs—
He couldn't play hide-and-seek.
Even a girl would be better than him.
Look, we've got to decide.
Let's take her on.
Hey, where's she gone . . . ?
Oh, she's gone back to their side.'

Eric Finney

Running Commentary

And Gazza kicks off. To Giggs.
It's Owen to Cole.
McManaman to me—
    and back off the wall.

Le Saux to Shearer.
Ferguson's fouled.
The play's waved on—
    and back off the wall.

Di Canio to Dublin.
To Yorke. I trap the ball.
To Casiraghi—
    and back off the wall.

I pass to Ronaldo and then to Wright.
Le Tissier falls.
Collins collects—
    and back off the wall.

Southgate to Sutton.
Huckerby calls.
Then Izzet to Ince—
    and back off the wall.

Lee to Laudrup.
Zidane must score.
Zola sidefoots—
    and back off the wall.

Just minutes to go.
It looks like a draw.
When Bergkamp finds Beckham—
    and back off the wall.

I tackle one player.
And beat nine more.
Then chip the keeper—
    and watch as the ball

Shoots into the net
    We've scored! We've scored!
My best goal yet—
    Just hear the crowd roar.

And Gazza kicks off. To Giggs.
It's Owen to Cole.
McManaman to me—
    and back off the wall.

David Horner

Strip

He's got it.
It cost a lot
weeks of waiting and saving up,
Mum paying half and the rest
part of his Christmas present.

He's put it on
in the bedroom
for the very first time,
he's gone downstairs looking like everything
he ever wanted. Shining.

He's playing
better than ever,
he'll get picked for the team
if he keeps this up. Weeks
of wearing the strip,
Mum grabbing it off him to wash it.

One day out shopping
in town with Mum
he's into extra time
with the crowd roaring him on.
Two big boys shove ahead of him.

They're laughing.
Look at that idiot.
Doesn't he know they've got a new strip?

Helen Dunmore

An Older Sister's Curse Put On To Her Football-Crazy Younger Brother For Telling Their Parents That He Saw Her In The Park With Her Boyfriend After She'd Told Them She'd Been Studying In The Library

May all the goals he scores for the school
team be own goals

May he be substituted in every school
match by Emma Harris
  who will score a hat-trick every time

May his Predator boots turn bright pink
whenever he wears them

May his entire collection of football
magazines turn into
  Ponies Forever magazines

May all his Power Play football figures
turn into Barbie dolls

May he never complete his 'Superstars of
    World Soccer' card collection

and when all this has happened and he believes that
    nothing else bad could possibly happen to him

May Mum forget that his autographed Man. U
shirt (personally signed by every member
    of the 1993–94 FA Cup Winners and League
        Champions squad, including
        the signatures of Eric Cantona,
            Ryan Giggs, Paul Ince, and Mark Hughes)
            should never,
                never ever
                    be washed . . .

. . . Oh YES!

Tony Langham

Trial Run

They spent the day at school
(part of Some Health Ed. project)
this bunch of blind kids;
showed us their speaking computers,
braille keyboards and books.

They were ace, but the most
amazing thing of all
was the football game they demo'd
out on the field that afternoon.

Sure, they could hear
the special ball, the coach's call
—but I mean
how can you *really* play footie
when you can't see a thing at all?
But they did.

Next day in the garden
I put a budgie bell inside
an old ball, sealed it back up,
tied my 'United' scarf round my eyes,
placed the ball on the lawn and tapped.

Tap—tap—tap—
                    it was weird,
like I had three feet.
Tried a dribble, a run, struggled
to keep on the ball,
concentrating, needing
to think all the time
which direction I'd sent it in.
Hell, was I slow!

Heard Dad's voice:
'*Here, son—to you!*'
I strained to home in my ears
to the bell, held my breath;
caught it on the instep,
booted it back
with a yell.

I can't begin to tell you
just what it was like,
how—exactly—it felt.
It's so different, the sound
the feel of the ball
when you can't see;
almost as if
it's inside you.

Patricia Leighton

Give Us Our Ball Back, Missus

Give us our ball back, missus
it landed in your yard
and broke your garden gnome
but we didn't kick it hard.

Give us our ball back, missus
we won't do it again
but it wasn't me that shot it
through your greenhouse window pane.

Give us our ball back, missus
didn't mean to hit that shirt,
the white one hanging out to dry
now stained with mud and dirt.

Give us our ball back, missus
we'll play somewhere else instead
but it was him who volleyed it
and hit your poodle's head.

Give us our ball back, missus
just this one last time.
Oh no, don't lock it in your shed
because it isn't mine.

Aw, missus, that's not fair
cos we have to go home soon
and anyway we're coming back
next Saturday afternoon.

Paul Cookson

It's All The Fault Of Those Football Magazines

I cut out photos of football stars
    and stick them on my wall.
There's so many now, you can hardly see
    the wallpaper at all.

My mum says I must have spent a fortune
    with all the ones I've got.
I lie and watch them kicking or heading
    or running to take a shot.

As long as I can see them there,
    everything is quite all right,
but it's a very different story
    as soon as I turn out the light.

The footballers don't stay on the wall—
    they jump down and come alive.
I can hear the excited shouts of the crowd
    as the goalkeeper takes a dive.

I can hear the referee's whistle blow
 and thuds as the players pass.
I can sense the ball fly overhead
 and smell the earth and grass.

Sometimes I feel the heat of their bodies
 the footballers get so near,
but every time I open my eyes
 they instantly disappear.

Then when I turn to go to sleep
 they start all over again.
'Why are you still awake?' calls Dad,
 but how can I explain?

Charles Thomson

Dream Team

My team
Will have all the people in it
Who're normally picked last.

Such as me.

When it's my turn to be chooser
I'll overlook Nick Magic-Feet-Jones
And Supersonic Simon Hughes

And I'll point at my best friend Sean
Who'll faint with surprise
And delight.

And at Robin who's always the one
Left at the end that no one chose—
Unless he's away, in which case it's guess who?

And Tim who can't see a thing
Without his glasses.
I'll pick him.

And the rest of the guys that Mr Miller
Calls dead-legs but only need their chance
To show what they're made of.

We'll play in the cup final
In front of the class, the school, the town,
The world, the galaxy.

And due to the masterly leadership shown
By their captain, not forgetting
His three out-of-this-world goals,

We'll WIN.

Frances Nagle

My Worst Nightmare

I had a terrible nightmare
I woke up in a sweat,
with my heart really racing
and my clothes ringing wet.

I dreamt there was no football,
not one game in the land,
for, in my worst dream of all time,
football had been banned.

The stadiums had been closed
the pitches all dug up,
old ladies now grew flowers
inside the great World Cup.

Footballs had been flattened,
and mascots set quite free,
all football players without a job
were sent away to sea.

The whole thing was a disaster;
my worst nightmare of all,
for what would we ever do
in a world without football?

Andrew Collett

We'll Support You Evermore

Blue is the Colour

Blue is the colour
Football is the game,
We're flippin freezing
Cos we're watching in the rain,
Our team is naff,
But we still remain,
Cos football, football is the game.

Richard Caley

The Fan

I've got my lucky jacket on
I haven't brushed my hair
I've even bought my programme from
    That lucky seller there.

At half time we'll change places if
    We haven't scored by then
And I will sit with Grandad
And Dad will sit with Ben.

I haven't worn my scarf, not since
    We lost five nil, away,
But I really like this T-shirt . . .
    I hope we win today.

Petonelle Archer

Then and Now

I've supported the green and white
since they were great
(and while they were . . . rubbish).

I've supported the green and white
since they were in black-and-white
on television.

I've supported the green and white
since the ground was a graveyard
for people, not hopes.

I've supported the green and white
since they had mutton-chop whiskers
not contracts with L'Oréal.

I've supported the green and white
since they brought home silverware
not just cheques.

And I'll support the green and white
whether they win or lose
tonight.

Tom Wilde

Saturday Night Blues

What do I care for the telly?
Why should I want to play?
What do I care for a story at bedtime
when my team lost today?

Fred Sedgwick

Weak End

End of the match.
Lost. Feeling bitter.
Crowd all gone home.
Ground covered with litter.

Floodlights switched off.
Flags all lie dead.
Birds peck at worms.
Players in bed.

Sad home supporters
Unable to speak,
Dreaming, and hoping
For better next week.

John Kitching

GOAL!

Yes!
hands
fly
from
our
pockets
like
angels
we
leap
for the sun
and fall happily back to earth.

John Coldwell

Oi, Ref!

Oi, Ref!
You blind or what?
Can't you see!
That should've been
A Penalty!

Oi, Ref!
Do me a favour!
You make me sick!
That should've been
A direct Free Kick!

Oi, Ref!
Get a life!
You'd better run'n'hide!
That goal
Was definitely Off-Side!

Oi, Ref!
What's happened to
y'whistle?
It's no wonder we all howl.
Send off that defender!
That was a Blatant Foul!

Oi, Ref!
Well done! Great game!
Three–one for us.
You did just fine.
Y'can come back here
And ref for us
Anytime!!!

Tony Langham

City Fan

There's only one team for me.
My pals say it's a pity.
Well, I can't help that:
I support City.

Why don't you switch
To United, they say.
Spent millions on a striker
Only yesterday.

Or swap to Rangers—
They won the cup;
Or Rovers: they're a team
On the up-and-up.

Rangers or Rovers . . .
Or even Athletic.
But City . . . well,
They're just pathetic.

Manager's terrible.
They're a hopeless lot.
And haven't they just
Lost ten on the trot?

It's all true what they say—
City do seem fated:
Ended up last season
Relegated.

I suppose it's all about
Loyalty.
I have this feeling
It's down to me.

It's Saturday. Raining.
Where's my anorak?
I'm off to see City.
They'll be back.

Eric Finney

The Away Supporter

Right in the middle of the visitors' stand,
The solitary supporter with a banner in his hand.

The last loyal voice to cheer on his side,
The others got married, gave up, or died.

He shouts and yells as his team lose again
Then hurries away to catch the last train.

John Coldwell

The Stranger

He was shouting,
Red in the face and shouting.
Arms thrashing,
Waving aggression,
Arguing loudly
With men who were
Arguing loudly.

Pushing with prejudice,
Almost fighting,
Deaf to pleading.

Who was this exploding stranger
Who had said he would protect;
Who had promised the treat
And his company?

Taking sides,
Swearing, jostling,
Threatening more . . .
Anger grown out of singing,
Turning to hatred of different colours.

'Be polite and kind.'
'Put yourself in their shoes.'
'A smile costs nothing.'
'Respect others.'

Lessons from another world
Before the madness of the match
Transformed my dad.

Daphne Kitching

39

I'm a Football Yob

I'm a football yob,
I'm a football yob,
An' I've got a great big belly
An' I've got a great big gob.

I've got a tattooed forehead
With the message, 'Up the Reds'
An' I've got some steel-capped dockers
Just for kicking in some heads.

I like to smash up buses
And I like to smash up trains,
Cos I'm big and brave and fearless—
And I haven't any brains.

Clive Webster

A Game of Two Halves

As the game kicked off	so did the fight
Our team won a corner	a gang got us cornered
Their keeper punched the ball clear	their leader punched me on the ear
A free kick to the reds	three kicks to the head
Sliced through the defence	a knife through the fence
The number one dived right	another one went down
The ball hit the back of the net	his face hit the deck
The ref raised his hand	the police took a stand
A red card for foul play	a red hand for foul play
A player sent off on a stretcher	a fan sent off in an ambulance
Our boys won one–nil	their boys had a different goal in mind

Tom Wilde

A Kick in the Teeth

Dear Dino,
Welcome.
Just what City needs.
Now our dream, the Double,
Can come true.
I've stuck some pictures of you
On my wall,
Would love (hint, hint)
To have one more.
   Yours,
     Anne
       (Your Greatest Fan)

Oh, Dino, thank you,
It's tremendous. Life-size!
I've stuck it next to
Where I lay my head.
Great game on Saturday—
How fast you ran.
City for the Cup!
All thanks to you.
   With Love,
     Your devoted Anne

My Dearest Dino,
When you smiled at me
At the Leicester game
Just before you scored
For the second time,
I felt so proud.
Last thing each night
I kiss your photograph.
Sleep tight, my darling.
    Anne,
        With all my love

Dino, you can't!
WE need you HERE.
If I can't see you play
I know I'll die.
Oh, Dino, money
Isn't everything.
Change your mind
OR I'LL RIP UP
YOUR PHOTOGRAPH.
    I mean it.
        Anne

PS Before you leave,
Please get me
Pellini's photo. Signed.

Frances Nagle

Saturday

Dear Diary

Saw my first match today.
Pompey vs. Man. City at Fratton Park.
A wet Saturday afternoon.
Very wet.

Old men with meat pies
and damp newspapers.
Young men with scarves and attitudes.
We were in the cheap seats,
perched like eagles above
the luminous green rectangle.
An island of grass in Portsmouth's
grey concrete.
I read my programme, unable
to find any famous names.

The match was dismal.
City scored before half-time.
I waited for the replay,
expecting Des Lynam's comments.
Was that it?
A moment of disaster, and then
just the restart?

The second half was worse.
I needed the loo
but didn't dare move.
The crowd was wet and bored.
The players were wet and bored.
Nobody scored.
Pompey's fans drifted away
booing and whistling.
We waited for the referee
to whistle too.

Beaten one—nil at home.
Tragic.

Can't wait till Saturday!

Tom Wilde

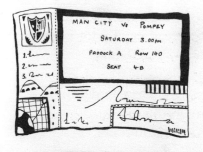

'Villa-nelle

If only I could play for Aston Villa,
I've got the kit—the claret and the blue,
I'd quash the opposition like Godzilla.

Every game would be a real thriller,
I'd show them how to score a goal or two,
If only I could play for Aston Villa.

The fans would find a nickname like 'Gorilla'
For me, as the pitch became a zoo.
I'd quash the opposition like Godzilla.

Their goalie would be crying in his pillow,
I'd make him think he hadn't got a clue,
If only I could play for Aston Villa.

They'd look at me and say, 'Here comes The Killer,'
Though I might get shown a red card, that is true,
As I quashed the opposition like Godzilla.

But, for now, I'll lick my strawberry and vanilla
Ice-lolly, while I'm waiting in the queue
To see the lads that play for Aston Villa
Quash the opposition like Godzilla.

Celia Warren

I'm For . . .

I'm for the team that's fast and clean
not dirty or mean, I'm for the team
that doesn't stop running
whose passes are stunning
and the ball seems to know
just where it should go
to fall smooth and neat
at the next twitching feet
as they sweep down the pitch
switching wings as they race
to make space or run rings
round an outpaced defence. I'm for
the team whose strength is skill,
that will twist and swerve
with control and nerve
as they dribble through the middle
but don't fiddle, fight, or quibble
with the ref
wasting time and breath. I'm
for the team who play so well
that my mind and heart

are lost in their art
so I don't scream or yell
but gasp in delight and grin.
(I don't care if they win.)

Dave Calder

Why Did He Do That, Dad?

The score was nil–nil; five minutes to go,
Both teams flat out for the winner.
On the attack came Rovers again,
The ball flashed out to Joe Skinner.

Round a defender, a swerve to his right
The striker bore down on the goal.
Back came his foot, keeper rushed out,
His foot under Joe's boot sole.

'Crack' was heard around the ground,
The goalie's face went ashen.
Skinner was left with an open goal,
'Score!' yelled the crowd with passion.

But Joe was made of finer stuff.
He hadn't a moment of doubt.
Broken leg, he thought and turned
And hacked the ball far out.

Over the touchline it went for a throw,
A certain goal ignored.
Strange—peculiar silence,
Then forty thousand roared.

Boy in the stand, said to his father,
'Why'd he do that, Dad?'
Arm round shoulder, caring hug,
'Because he's a sportsman, lad!'

Redvers Brandling

Football Crazy

Grounds for Recollection

(An old footballer remembers)

'Do you remember *Anfield*?' he asked.
Old Trafford nodded his head.
'She lived down near the *Maine Road*
By *St Andrew's* church,' he said.

'*Molineux* her too,' he said,
'They went to *St James's* school.
They once pretended to find a *Goldstone*.
They were always playing the fool.

'They tore down *The Shed* and built *The New Den*
In *The Dell* by *The Riverside*.
They used sticks they took from *The Hawthorns*
And *Turf* from the *Moor* inside.

'Once for a lark, in *Goodison Park*,
They made all of us boys go trembly
By claiming they'd found on the *City's Ground*
A Cup Final ticket for *Wembley*!'

John Foster

A Soccer Star Narrowly Missed

A soccer star narrowly missed
The goal, and was grieved to be hissed
    So he broke down in tears
    To ironic cheers
Cos he'd hoped to be cuddled and kissed.

Joseph D. Knight

Hairless Half-Back

Why hasn't that player got any hair?
Has he played too many headers?
Or is he just footballed?

Pam Gidney

The Match Ball

No one scored a goal with me,
No one celebrated.
No one wanted to keep me,
I feel a bit deflated.

Mike Jubb

Last Word

Said the pitch
to the grandstand,
'I'm old and I'm lined;
Life seems so flat
After all these years.'

Said the grandstand
to the pitch,
'Well, never mind;
I'm so unhappy
My seats are in tiers.'

Trevor Millum

53

Goalpost Blues

Who'd be a football goalpost?
Nobody with any sense.
I've been one for twenty years.
I wish I'd become a fence.

I get kicked and banged and thumped—
but do I get any thanks?
No—I'm just grabbed and shaken.
I should've been sawn into planks.

No one asked me what I wanted.
They didn't listen when I yelled.
Next time I'll be something else
when it's my turn to be felled.

An orange box or floorboard,
a door frame or a tea chest.
I'm not fussy what I do—
though I've one small request.

Don't turn me into a goalpost.
I hate being kicked in the shins.
I'm not trying to be awkward
but does it really matter who wins?

Janis Priestley

Basil Bragg

You may have heard of Basil Bragg
Who earns his living as a corner flag.
When Saturday home games come around
You'll find him down at the City Ground.
In the dressing room, as he makes the switch
From a human being to part of the pitch,
He really is a startling sight
In a body stocking painted white.
His tiny flag in Forest red
He screws down firmly in his head,
Then takes his place at a quarter to three—
A vital appurtenance is Basil B.
His brother Bert, so keen on horses,
Is a winning post at the major courses.

To those who fancy sporting action—
Unusual posts bring satisfaction.

Jack Ousbey

The Trainer's Magic Sponge

I'm the trainer's magic sponge,
I'm brought on to ease
ankles, feet and toes and shins,
heads and necks and backs and knees.

I'm the trainer's magic sponge
soaking aches and pains.
Just one touch is all I need
curing suspect strains.

I'm the trainer's magic sponge,
the smallest member of the team.
A wonder-working miracle,
unsung hero, never seen.

Paul Cookson

Cross

'The extraordinary thing about footballers,'
Said the cross Man in Green,
'Is that they should always want to be eleven,
DON'T INTERRUPT ME, each side, I mean.'

'I can understand twenty-two playing football,
Good healthy fun
To kick the ball in and out of touch . . . PLEASE
DON'T MAKE FACES . . .
But couldn't it be done by nine or twenty-one?'

'KINDLY DON'T INTERRUPT ME if I point out
That this is a game
In which always being eleven is ridiculous.
Why should the numbers always be the same?'

'Wouldn't it be much more interesting
If nobody were to know
How many footballers were going to play,
And let this silly notion of eleven go?
What do you say? Eh?'

Crossly the Man in Green said,
'All I get is INTERRUPTION
    AND SILLY FACES, just as I feared.
I may as well kick myself into touch!'
And out in the long grass he disappeared.

John Pudney

Football Out-Of-Focus

NEWSFLASH ...
        NEWSFLASH ...
                NEWSFLASH ...

Good afternoon. Welcome to
Football Out-of-Focus.
This is Dennis Linehamup reporting.

We have just received this newsflash.
Within the last half hour the teams
have been announced for the
annual Nouns v. Verbs Football Final.
However, the selectors are not quite sure
about the suitability of some of those
selected and would welcome suggestions
for substitutes. Here are
the provisional selections:

Noun Namers	Verb Action United
1 A. Ball	1 W. E. Kick
2 N. U. Strip	2 I. Swear
3 R. Fans	3 U. Shout
4 F. Lags	4 H. E. Dives
5 F. A. Cup	5 M. O. Wins
6 X. I. Players	6 Will Dribble
7 W. E. R. Best-Team	7 S. Hoots
8 K. Ickoff	8 C. M. Score
9 R. Penalty	9 U. R. Fouling
10 L. Ines-Man	10 R. Gue
11 R. E. Feree	11 S. U. P. Porting

Please feel free to make your own selection of
players and send them to:

Football Out-Of-Focus
c/o The Person In Charge
Wherever You Are
FUT BA11.

Daphne Kitching

Club Call

(Extracts from an A–Z of Football Club Anagrams)

Al earns
Ava's Not Ill!
Bye Dry Count!
Dem blowin'
Dire Alien Cults
Don Wins Nowt!
Hum, Alf!
Ill over op.
Lad ends run
Man Shot Other Putt
Nice Hen Made Trust
Nothing from a test
Real new car axed
Spot hot rum
Veer Not!
Vole Trap
War! Witches Bomb Lion!
We unlace dentist!
Whip cost win

John Foster

Answers on page 128

Football (a double acrostic)

Footballers who foul will be sent ofF.

Often they leave to a loud boO.

Or, worse, ironic cheers as they gO.

Top players need a steady temperamenT.

Body fitness is essential: no flaB.

Arsenal can be as boring as SiberiA.

Left wingers dribble with the balL.

Last minute shot can mean a goaL!

Wes Magee

Three Football Haiku

Winter Game
A pack of dark wolves
eagerly hunting the ball.
Their breath is misty.

Goalkeeper
Our forwards attack.
I stand and tread the soft turf,
patiently waiting.

Goal
Across the wide town—
the roar of a bomb bursting:
the ball hits the net.

Tony Mitton

In The
Good Old Days

The Man Who Invented Football

The man who invented football,
He must have been dead clever,
He hadn't even a football shirt
Or any clothes whatever.

The man who invented soccer,
He hadn't even a *ball*
Or boots, but only his horny feet
And a bison's skull, that's all.

The man who invented football,
To whom our hats we doff,
Had only the sun for a yellow card
And death to send him off.

The cave-mouth was the goal-mouth,
The wind was the referee,
When the man who did it did it
In 30,000 BC!

Kit Wright

The Game's Afoot!

A Diary Entry
July 31st AD 1579

Yestere'en myself and good fellows all
Made merry an hour, at my contrivance,
Which did our idleness dispense.

Seeing hog's offal that our scullion did dispose,
The bladder I didst obtain and by breath of mouth
This thing didst I inflate.
To constrain its airy fullness,
With twine I loop'd and tied the neck.
And lo! I had a jester's ball that made a merry bounce.

My cousin attending our dwelling, did call,
'How now, good Will! What shape of plaything is this?'
By explanation I didst kick the hog-ball to his proximity,
Which he, in like fashion, didst immediate return.

Our rumpus, jests, and jocund laughter
Brought many a local youth envious to our place,
Who didst entreat our game to share.

65

Then with cheery sport our newmade ball
Was kick'd from lad to laughing lad.
One such clodpole eschewing his foot's employment
Didst nod the ball with good direction.

This variance we didst applaud and thereon
Rul'd to catch-not nor hand this bauble,
But, by skill and practice, to apply solely
Our foot and head's dexterity.

Tutor Thomas, hearing our shrill cacophony
Call'd cease to our extemporary play,
Suggesting fine order of such makeshift sport.

As two and twenty lads had now conven'd,
Thomas, by count, did split our company in twain.
'Now!' he cried. 'Get thee unto the orchard!
Where convivial battle shall ensue.'

Designating two pippin trees, some pikeshaft apart,
  proclaimed,
'Your goal will be to foot this ball
Betwixt these standards.
Your friendly protagonists, the while,
Defending so, against your onslaughts,
Must hatch such contrivance as to achieve the goal
  themselves.'

So, the field was set. The battlelines enscrib'd.
Our tendons taut, our muscles abulge to anticipate the off,
Then to start the game of playe—
Good Thomas did blast upon a shrill pipe—one, two, and
  three!
Then thrice did shout—

'Here goest we!'

David Whitehead

England v. Germany

25 December 1914

The men were dug in trenches
and snow lay on the ground,
machine guns and sandbags
and barbed wire all around.

The Englishmen in one trench
faced Germans in another
on Christmas Day, and all
were far from home and mother.

Two nations in a conflict
we call The First World War
with weapons of destruction
never seen before.

But though the men were enemies
it was Christmas Day after all.
Some joined in singing a hymn,
and some began to call:

'Happy Christmas, Tommy!'
'Fritz, Happy Christmas to you!'
and some even met to swap presents,
as the friendly feeling grew.

Then something remarkable happened
that the generals hadn't planned.
The enemy soldiers shook hands
in the deadly no-man's land.

Something extraordinary happened—
it was Christmas Day after all—
the soldiers put down their rifles
and began to play football.

We don't know who won the toss,
or even if they tossed.
We don't know how long the match was.
We don't know who won or lost.

We don't know who played centre-forward
or who took the goalie's role.
We don't even know for that matter
if they bothered to have a goal.

We just know some men in Khaki
and some others wearing grey
stopped the war and kicked a ball
in the snow on Christmas Day.

It could have ended the hatred,
the killing and the pain,
but the High Commands decreed
it must never happen again.

So the men hid once more with machine guns,
behind sandbags and barbed wire
and instead of 'Happy Christmas'
the officers called, 'Open fire'.

Two of the men who'd swapped presents,
shaken hands, and smiled when they met,
met again, and one stabbed the other
to death with a bayonet.

Charles Thomson

Footy in the Street

When we were young and fanciful
The game was played for fun
No 442 or 433
Just kick the ball and run.

Like actors we rehearsed our parts
And acted out the roles
No Stadium of Light for us
Discarded coats our goals.

Our floodlights were a street lamp
The North Stand was some trees
The roaring crowd, a passing car
No need for referees.

Football was so simple then
With every kid a winner
At end of play we trudged off home
To wash and scrub for dinner.

At night we talked of scoring goals
For our favourite teams
We longed to be back out there
On our concrete field of dreams.

Richard Caley

Come Saturday

Come Saturday,
The whole town comes alive.
People are going one way,
From all the streets,
They are going the one way,
And meeting and joining,
And going on and meeting more and more
Till the trickle becomes a flood.
And men are so packed tight
That the cars have to nose their way through.
And you come to the stadium,
And it's humming,
A hum comes from the bowl.
And the people inside seem to be saying,
Come on in, come on in,
And you jostle at the turnstile,
And the turnstile clicks and clicks,
And you push nearer and nearer,
Through the dark gap,
Then you're in.
And the great stand of the City end,
It's like a hall,
A great hall,
And you go on.

Through the arch
And you see the pitch,
Green, new shaven and watered,
And the groundsman's made the white lines,
As straight as a ruler,
And the ash is pressed.
And you find your place among the fans,
The real fans,
The singers and chanters and rattle wavers.
And a sheet of tobacco smoke hangs over the crowd.
And the crowd whistles and hoots,
And the policemen circling the pitch
Look up and know they're in for a rough day of it,
And the stadium fills up,
The Open End first, then the City End,
Then the paddock, then the covered seated stand,
Then, last of all, the fat directors
With the Lord Mayor and cigars.
And the reporters are in their little glass box,
And the cameramen position themselves
By the goal,
And there's a looking down the tunnel,
Then a hush.
Then out they come.
The lads,
Like toy footballers on a green billiard table.
And the roar goes up . . .

City City, City City,
We'll support you evermore,
We'll support you evermore.
City City, City City,
We'll support you evermore,
We'll support you evermore.

Peter Terson

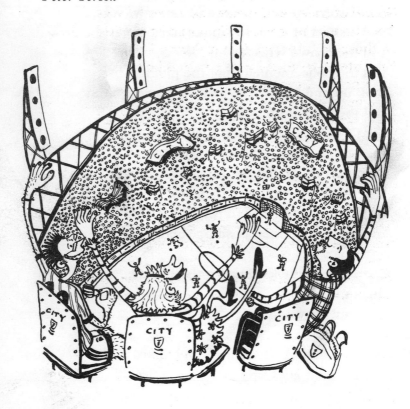

Stan

'The footballers of today,' our grandad said,
'Are spoilt and overpaid. You know my views.
But let me tell you about one of soccer's greats—
Players today aren't fit to clean his shoes.
I used to go and watch him with my dad,
Stan Matthews, on the right wing for Stoke;
So full of tricks and twists and turns he was,
You thought he'd vanish in a puff of smoke!
In those days he was just a skinny kid,
But listen—he could juggle with a ball
As if he'd got it tied on to his feet,
And once he had—no hurry then at all.
He'd walk the ball up to some poor full-back,
Weaving a sort of slow-motion magic spell,
Tempting him, daring him in to tackle,
And when he did, Stan's off like a young gazelle!
I've seen him dance and dribble with the ball,
Now slow, now fast, past six or seven men,
And then stop dead and let them all recover
And tease them dizzy—and beat them all again!'

'Are you sure, Grandad, it was six or seven?
Last time you told us it was two or three.'

'Well . . . three or four at least. But did I tell you
About Sir Stanley's finest match: Bolton v. —'

'—Blackpool. Yes, Grandad, you told us several times
And showed us that old Cup Final video too,
With all the players in long and baggy shorts.
But go on—no one tells it quite like you.'

'Well, Stanley played for Blackpool in those days:
Cup Final, nineteen fifty-three.
Bolton 3–1 ahead with twenty minutes left—
Blackpool dead and buried, you'd guarantee.
Matthews had had a quiet game till then
But now, just when all hope had nearly gone,
They slipped the ball to Stanley on the wing
To see if he could turn the magic on.
And of course he did: he ran and dribbled
Bolton out of sight—it's football history.
He laid the winner on in injury time
And Perry scored and Blackpool won 4–3.'

Eric Finney

Brazilian Footballer

Pelé kicked in his mother's belly!
And the world shouted:
Gooooooooooooooooooooooooooooooooal!
When her son was born,
He became the sun,
And rolled on the fields of heaven.
The moon and stars trained and coached him,
In the milky way
He swayed, danced and dribbled,
Smooth like water off a duck's back
Ready always to attack.
One hot day, heaven fell down, floored!
Through the Almighty's hands
Pelé had scored!

Faustin Charles

Bobby Charlton

like this: head up, looking where he was going
just as you were supposed to, but always
changing direction, slightly, now this
way, now that, no more than needed so that
obstructions do not have to be met
are not there, simply:
                              a kind of cunning
for a shy man, nothing as artless as contact,
evasion was mannerly:
                              head up,
knowing where he was, where the others were
what they were doing, and changing the pattern
with the same flowing unhastening stride:
head up, shoulders back, leaning from the toes,
the same stride with the conscious grace gone
that used to bring him bending in from his wing,
faded into something better, at the centre, experienced
making connections from such a distance . . .

Confluence, influence, with the same flow, although
older, slower, the moments were fewer;
one of the best, and better than some of the best,
as good as he could be, and then at last
a refinement of all that he had been: like that.

Brian Lee

End Game

'The Busby Babes'—
That's what they called them;
And everyone in Manchester knew
They were 'on line' for the Cup.

But that fatal day
At Munich Airport
Made football history
Of a different kind.

Now, from the newspaper cuttings of '58,
Their hairstyles look strange
And their faces somehow older,
Forever trapped in another age—
Forever dreaming of the fame
        they hoped would come.

Trevor Harvey

Great-Grandpa's Boots Remember . . .

Great-Grandpa's boots
are dry and dusty,
half-forgotten,
cracked and crusty,
hang behind the spare-room door,
don't get dubbined any more,
just dangle there, too old to play,
but not too old to sigh and say:

Ah, those were the days . . .
when football shorts
were long,
and referees
were rarely wrong,
and even football stars
had ordinary jobs
like mending cars
or digging holes . . .
Oh, where are the goals
of yesterday . . . ?

Who'd have thought
that football could become
more showbizness than sport?
What have they done
with all the fun
we used to have on Saturday afternoon?
They might as well be playing
on the moon!

Ah, if we could have it back
for just a game,
and be there waiting like we used to do
as that shrill blast of kick-off whistle blew
we'd show these Superstars
a thing or two.

We'd show them something great
that can't be bought:
We'd show them honest,
good old-fashioned . . . SPORT!

Tony Mitton

The Trouble with Grandad

Our grandad has a football scarf
And woolly football hat.
He likes to sing the football songs
And chat the football chat.
He likes to cheer the football cheer
And drink the football lager beer.

Six days a week and he's OK,
A well-behaved old thing.
But on the football Saturday
It's so embarrassing,
A quiet, silver-haired old man
Behaving like a football fan.

He stamps and yells and (oh, the shame)
He's even got a rattle.
I tell him how it's just a game.
He acts like it's a battle.
ARSENAL! ARSENAL FOR THE CUP!
Do grandads ever quite grow up?

John Whitworth

Up For the Cup

Wembley

Last night I had a thrilling dream
About Cup Final Day
As many thousands cheered their team,
Along the Wembley Way.

Some cheered the Reds, some cheered the Blues,
Towards those towers ahead,
And neither side believed they'd lose,
They'd rather die instead.

I clutched my ticket in my hand
As I approached the ground;
Inside I heard a big brass band,
A fine majestic sound.

And when at last I reached my place
The time was half-past two;
Excitement showed on every face,
Supporting Red or Blue.

At ten to three the teams came out
To one tremendous roar,
The greatest thrill without a doubt,
I've ever known before.

At kick-off time I felt the noise,
It seemed to shake the ground,
As men and women, girls and boys,
Made one fantastic sound.

Each goal came under fierce attack
As shots were fired galore,
It seemed as though one side must crack,
Yet neither team could score.

The second half was just the same,
But near the end of play,
Of what had been a thrilling game,
Our striker got away.

He beat three men before he steered
The ball into the net,
And our supporters cheered and cheered,
A goal I won't forget.

But most of all I was so sad
When Mummy woke me up,
Because you see it was my dad,
Whose goal had won the cup.

Roland Egan

Cup-Final

T. O'Day

W. E. March   T. O. G. Lory
J. Usty   O. Uwait   N. See

G. O'Dow
A. Day   W. Ewill   N. Infa H. I. Story

Young   N. Fast   M. O'Reskill   I. T. Sreally
W. Egot

A. L. L. Sewnup   W. E. Rethel   A. D. S. Whollrun

A. Round   W. Embley

W. I. Thecup

Roger McGough

A Tour of Wembley

We went on a tour of Wembley.
It was twenty pounds for four.
We joined the end of the queue
and the guide showed us in through the door.

We went into the control room
to see what Security sees—
every part of the stadium
was shown on rows of TVs.

We went to the England changing room
and I sat in the goalkeeper's seat
and I thought what it felt like to be there
in victory and defeat.

We lined in the player's tunnel.
The guide played the crowd's loud roar
through the speakers. I knew one day
I'd be there for real for sure.

We stood by the Royal Box
and then our team walked up.
I stood where the winners stand
and the guide gave me the cup.

I could see the cheering fans—
and then they were gone in a blink.
I got a souvenir book
and Dad bought me a fizzy drink.

Charles Thomson

The Road to Wembley

Imagine the scene.
It's Wembley, the stadium,
sometime in the Future.
A hundred thousand spectators
are going wild
as two teams hammer
it out for the FA Cup.

The match is being transmitted
all over the world,
via satellite and cable.
So about two hundred million
people are watching
as one of the goalkeepers
punts the ball upfield,
having just pulled off
a spectacular save
from a hand-scorching shot.

The ball comes down
in the mid-field
where the latest
19-year-old superstar
from the North-East
expertly chests it down,

89

swivels like a dancer
and chips a fabulous ball
over the heads
of the on-rushing
opposition players.

His touch is perfect
and the ball lands
at the feet
of a veteran striker
who's playing his last game
in his final season.

He takes the ball
to the edge of the box,
lifts it on the move
and hits a volley
which zaps past
the despairing hands
of the keeper.

GOAL!

The cry echoes
around the stadium
and in every room

all over the world,
wherever the match
is being watched.

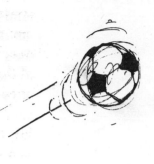

And as the ball
hits the back
of the net,
the striker
salutes the crowd

and remembers
at that precise moment,
remembers another goal
he scored in exactly
the same way
almost twenty years
earlier on a muddy pitch
one wet winter Wednesday
in a Junior Schools
League match.

He remembers
how he imagined then
that he had just scored
the winning goal
in the FA Cup Final.

and remembers too
all the matches
he's played in,
remembers every win,
every defeat,
all the injuries,
all the pain,
remembers each
and every season,
remembers everything

and smiles secretly
to himself,
just before
his team-mates
rush up and bury
him under their
congratulating
bodies.

Like they say:
it's a long, hard road
to Wembley.

Tony Langham

World Cup

Paul Higgins

93

HORROR REPLAY

'Play it again, Sam!'
I tell my younger brother,
When Mum and Dad have gone to bed;
And he rewinds the videotape
Back to the spot
Where on freeze-frame and forward play
Is the scene that always scares
Us half to death!
Its sheer and utter fright
Keeps us both awake at night!
The shrieking and the screaming
Is the stuff for terror-dreaming!

And sitting in the lounge
So late at night
My brother and I relive,
As often as we wish,
The FULL SHOCK and TOTAL HORROR
Of the moment when,
From a VICIOUS KICK,
The ball goes into the back
Of the England net.

Trevor Harvey

Subutteo Sam

Subutteo Sam is a tiny little man
With a seam running right down his head
He lives in a box with the rest of the team
At the bottom of little Tommy's bed.

With a spin and a flick
He's made to kick
A ball the size of a marble
All the crowd can do
When Sammy's on the ball
Is sit back in wonder and marvel.

He's the star attraction
With his goal-mouth action
He's a right little pocket-sized hero
Although not very tall, he's a wizard on the ball
And he swiftly makes the score ten–zero.

He likes to dazzle and amaze
As he glides across the baize
He is Pelé's moulded, painted, plastic son
He stands proudly on his base
As he's put back in the case
With yet another Cup Final won.

Richard Caley

It's a Funny Old Game

A Manager's Tale

At the start of the season
we were third from the top
now we need these points
to avoid the drop.

We'd win this match
I'd sworn on oath
it was a game of two halves
but we lost them both.

As manager here
I must take the blame
as I've said before
it's a funny old game.

I'm as sick as a parrot
what more can I say?
The lads done good
but it wasn't our day.

We'll be back next season
just wait and see
the players, the fans
and hopefully me.

Richard Caley

97

One to Eleven — Football Speak

'It's a game of two halves,'
said the pundit knowingly.
'And?' I enquired.
'One pitch, three officials,
four goalposts and two crossbars.
Five penalties, when there's a shoot-out,
And, in the old days, five forwards
And five defenders.
Plus, of course, the goalkeeper,
Which makes six.'
'I see,' I said.
'And I suppose the crowd
Is in seventh heaven
When their team scores.'
'That's right,' said the pundit.
'Number 8 is the inside right,
Or was. Nowadays he could be
Either in midfield or a striker.'
'But number 9's always
The centre forward,' I said.
'Yes, though they'll tell you:
There's only one Alan Shearer.

There's eleven players on each side,
Unless one gets a red card,
Then they're down to ten men.
And the tenth team in the Premiership
Is bottom of the top half.'
'Oh,' I said. 'What about the manager?'
'He's on his own,' said the pundit.
'Unless his team do the double,
Then he's one in a million.'

John Foster

There's Only One Michael Owen!

Why is it that football commentators
Often refer to players
As though there are several of them?
They go on about
'the likes of your Michael Owens.'
Don't they realize
THERE'S ONLY ONE MICHAEL OWEN!
Have they been watching
so many replays of *that goal*
that they've started to suffer
from double vision?

John Foster

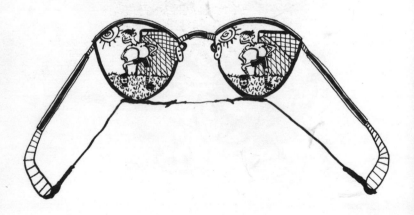

Goal Difference

with	success
weigh	heavy
the	top
teams	at
but	the
the	table
climb	up
needed	to
the	results
to	get
is	on
the	pressure
the	league
bottom	of
At	the

Coral Rumble

Professional Footballer

I'm a professional footballer.
The fans all think I'm brill.
I'm well paid for my talent.
Rewarded for my skill.

I do the business.
Present me with a chance to score
—you can be sure
I will.

Because I'm a professional footballer
and will keep on playing until
the fans no longer cheer me
or the Boss says I'm over the hill.

I do the business.
Five minutes into any game
I take aim
—one–nil!

Off the field I'm active.
I suppose my will is weak.
I can't resist the high life.
Love dancing cheek to cheek
with TV stars and models,
the glamorous and the chic.

That's show biz!
And, yes, it is expensive but
I soon foot
the bill
because I'm a professional footballer,
a striker with money to spare.
These days sport's my business
and I'm a millionaire.

(Yet my biggest thrill is still
when, five minutes into any game,
I take aim
—one–nil!)

Bernard Young

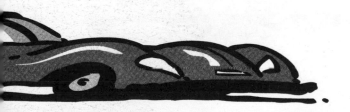

Hard Man

I kick
I elbow
I trip
I punch
I hack.

I am the very model
Of a modern centre back!

John Kitching

Pair of Hands Against Football

Opposition Supporters:	You make the cash-tills ring. You make crowds of people sing.
Goalkeeper's Supporters:	You make feet jump into a tackle then make them move into a dribble. Football—you draw a million eyes. Football—we love your ruses. You lead quick feet to strike and others to attack the strike to outsmart TWO HANDS— our GOALKEEPER'S HANDS.
Goalkeeper:	Well, artful ball from the grass, you shall not pass HANDS like wall for you football, stopping your triumph-roar cos I'm goalkeeper, you hear— HANDS OF TWO against eleven heads and feet of twenty-two
Opposition Supporters:	You make the crowd moan. You make the crowd go mean. You make the crowd leap up aggrieved. You make the crowd sit down relieved.

105

Goalkeeper's
Supporters: Come on zigzagging like a snake.
You find you have no gate!
Come on flying like a bird.
See—no cage for a bird!
Come straight like a bullet.
See—you're in HANDS like a wallet!

Goalkeeper: Well, artful ball from the grass,
you shall not pass
HANDS like wall
for you football,
stopping your triumph-roar
cos I'm goalkeeper, you hear—
HANDS OF TWO
against eleven heads and feet of
twenty-two

Opposition
Supporters: You make the crowd feel relaxed.
You make the crowd feel whacked.

Goalkeeper's
Supporters: You make a foot land you on a thigh,
make another drive you sky high,
make others turn you into a hare;
you come—our HANDS are there.
You bring a group, close, busy, like lions.
You get knocked up into HANDS of iron.

Goalkeeper: Well, artful ball from the grass,
                       you shall not pass
                       HANDS like wall
                       for you football,
                       stopping your triumph-roar
                       cos I'm goalkeeper, you hear—
                       HANDS OF TWO
                       against eleven heads and feet of
                            twenty-two.

Goalkeeper's   You make us feel washed up
Supporters: but roar at raised winner's cup.

Goalkeeper: Well, artful ball from the grass,
                       you shall not pass
                       HANDS like wall
                       for you football,
                       stopping your triumph-roar
                       cos I'm goalkeeper, you hear—
                       HANDS OF TWO
                       against eleven heads and feet of
                            twenty-two.

James Berry

Scoring a Goal

When I scored the winning goal
I had never felt so alone
The crowd went crazy, on their feet
But my heart sank like a stone
They say that scoring is marvellous,
The best feeling that's ever been known,
But it's hard to take
When you make a mistake
And the back of the net
Is your own.

Roger Stevens

Regrets

From where I sit
the roar of the crowd
is like distant thunder
shaking the ground.

It's lonely here
away from the fun,
the long pass, the short ball,
the cannon-fire shot,
shaking the goal.

Sitting here all alone
in the silent dressing room
with the ghosts of great players
is hard
I didn't mean to hit him
I lost my temper
and saw red—
the referee's red card.

Roger Stevens

Football Mad

Oh no, bless my soul!
Clever Trevor's scored a goal.

So he runs up the pitch
And wriggles his botty,
He is kissed by ten men
All sweaty and snotty,
Now he's waving his fist
To the Queen who just stares
The lad's going crazy
But everyone cheers.
Now what's he doing?
He's chewing the cud!
Now what's he doing?
He's rolling in mud!
Now he is crying
I think he's in pain
Now what's he doing?
He's smiling again.

Oh no, bless my soul
Clever Trevor's scored a goal.

He's doing gymnastics

He's doing some mime
He's kissing the ground
For a very long time,
He's now on his back
With his feet in the air
Now he's gone all religious
And stopped for a prayer.
Did he pray for the sick?
Did he pray for the poor?
No, he prayed for the ball
And he prayed to score.
No one but no one
Can re-start the game
Until Trevor has had
His moment of fame.

Oh no, bless my soul

Clever Trevor's scored a goal,
He kicked the ball into the net
How much money will he get?

Benjamin Zephaniah

Falling Star

When Danny had just learnt to crawl
His dad bought him his first football
He loved it.

Then he walked and got the trick
Of giving that big ball a kick
Terrific!

By the time he was four
He could dribble, pass, and score
Fantastic!

When everybody saw him play
They said *You'll be a star one day*
Believe it.

For Junior school and Sunday team
Danny played like a dream
Brilliant.

Top team scouts came to each game
Each of them thought just the same
Let's sign him.

He joined a club and very soon
They'd promised him the sun and moon
A future.

School slipped slowly out of sight
He thought of football day and night
Obsessive.

Youth team games were hard and tough
And Danny wasn't good enough
Disaster.

It broke his heart but it was true
His professional days were through
They dumped him.

Danny learned to smoke and swear
To show them that he didn't care
Who needs them?

Football's cruel, unforgiving
Not that many make a living
Ask Danny . . .

David Harmer

It Makes You Think

My dad gets paid just forty pounds
For every day he works,
Yet all the Premier footballers
Get more than that in perks.

Some of them, the papers say,
Get millions every year
For doing something that they love—
It's not a bad career!

And yet my dad works just as hard—
Harder, I suppose,
To see that money sloshing round
Just gets right up his nose.

So when I next see transfer fees
And wages that just stink,
I'll picture Dad and forty pounds—
It makes you stop and think.

Clive Webster

What My Uncle Billy Says

Footballers! They get away with murder,
earn more than is good for them,
swank about the place in flash cars,
Porsches, Beamers; get drunk,
pick fights in big posh discos,
some blonde bimbo always in tow;

cynically go where the money is,
Italy, Japan—or on telly advertising
stupid things like shower gel,
potato crisps. And on the field,
spitting, swearing, and pulling at
other players' shirts to get the ball;

and then, when they score, hugging
and kissing, rolling round like acrobats.
He'd pay them what factory workers get,
no more no less!

And all because I said I wanted to play
For Liverpool . . . and he's an Evertonian!

Matt Simpson

The Old Football Player

We adopted an old footballer
From a mail order charity list.
He arrived a week last Saturday,
With a label round his wrist,

Which said he'd played for Everton
Until 1984,
When they signed a younger player
And couldn't use him any more.

His career had travelled downhill—
Divisions one and two and three.
Then to a part-time park side
For whom he played without a fee.

He sadly stood before us
In his faded football kit,
Muddy boots, grubby socks,
And shorts that didn't fit.

Since then, he's been quite handy.
With dusters, mops, and brooms.
He manages the washing up
And vacuums all the rooms.

We never mention football
He seems to prefer it that way
And out of respect we change channels
When it's time for *Match of the Day*.

John Coldwell

Death of an Old Footballer

He was ready when the whistle blew
Laced up both his boots
Jumped up smiling from the bench
One of life's substitutes.

Raised his arm to the popular end
Flexed the suspect knee
And out of habit showed his studs
To the eternal referee.

Gareth Owen

Epitaph for Number Nine

Our centre forward's passing
Has been United's loss.
His final words were 'On me head'
So there we placed this cross.

Ian Whybrow

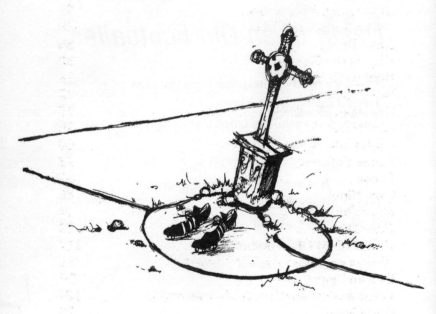

Index of Titles and First Lines
(First lines are in italics)

Index of Authors

Acknowledgements

The editor and publisher are grateful to the following for permission to publish their poems for the first time in this collection:

PETONELLE ARCHER: 'The Fan', copyright © Petonelle Archer 2000; ANN BONNER: 'Football', copyright © Ann Bonner 2000; REDVERS BRANDLING: 'Why Did He Do That, Dad?', copyright © Redvers Brandling 2000; DAVE CALDER: 'Rules of the Game', 'I'm For...', and 'Megaleague 3000', all copyright © Dave Calder 2000; FAUSTIN CHARLES: 'Brazilian Footballer', copyright © Faustin Charles 2000; JOHN COLDWELL: 'Goal', 'The Away Supporter', and 'The Old Football Player', all copyright © John Coldwell 2000; ANDREW COLLETT: 'Football Philosophy' and 'My Worst Nightmare', both copyright © Andrew Collett 2000; PAUL COOKSON: 'Give Us Our Ball Back, Missus' and 'The Trainer's Magic Sponge', both copyright © Paul Cookson 2000; ERIC FINNEY: 'Boys' Game?', 'City Fan', and 'Stan', all copyright © Eric Finney 2000; JOHN FOSTER: 'Club-Call', 'One to Eleven—Football Speak', and 'There's Only One Michael Owen', all copyright © John Foster 2000; PAM GIDNEY: 'Hairless Half-Back', copyright © Pam Gidney 2000; DAVID HARMER: 'Falling Star', copyright © David Harmer 2000; TREVOR HARVEY: 'End Game', copyright © Trevor Harvey 2000; DAVID HORNER: 'Running Commentary', copyright © David Horner 2000; MIKE JUBB: 'The Match Ball', copyright © Mike Jubb 2000; DAPHNE KITCHING: 'The Stranger' and 'Football Out-of-Focus', both copyright © Daphne Kitching 2000; JOHN KITCHING: 'Weak End' and 'Hard Man', both copyright © John Kitching 2000; TONY LANGHAM: 'An Older Sister's Curse Put On To Her Football Crazy Younger Brother', 'Oi, Ref!', and 'The Road to Wembley', all copyright © Tony Langham 2000; PATRICIA LEIGHTON: 'Trial Run', copyright © Patricia Leighton 2000; WES MAGEE: 'Football', copyright © Wes Magee 2000; TREVOR MILLUM: 'Last Word', copyright © Trevor Millum 2000; TONY MITTON: 'Football Haiku' and 'Great Grandpa's Boots Remember', all copyright © Tony Mitton 2000; JACK OUSBEY: 'Basil Bragg', copyright © Jack Ousbey 2000; JANIS PRIESTLEY: 'Goalpost Blues', copyright © Janis Priestley 2000; CORAL RUMBLE: 'Goal Difference', copyright © Coral Rumble 2000; FRED SEDGWICK: 'Saturday Night Blues', copyright © Fred Sedgwick 2000; MATT SIMPSON: 'What My Uncle Billy Says', copyright © Matt Simpson 2000; ROGER STEVENS: 'Scoring a Goal' and 'Regrets', both copyright © Roger Stevens 2000; CHARLES THOMSON: 'A Tour of Wembley', 'England v. Germany, 25 December 1914', 'It's All the Fault of Those Football Magazines', and 'Football for Beginners', all copyright © Charles Thomson 2000; CELIA WARREN: 'Villa-Nelle', copyright © Celia Warren 2000; CLIVE WEBSTER: 'I'm a Football Yob' and 'It Makes You Think', both copyright © Clive Webster 2000; DAVID WHITEHEAD: 'The Game's Afoot!', copyright © David Whitehead 2000; and TOM WILDE: 'Then and Now', 'A Game of Two Halves', and 'Saturday', all copyright © Tom Wilde 2000.

We are also grateful for permission to include the following previously published poems:

JAMES BERRY: 'Pair of Hands Against Football' from When I Dance (Puffin, 1988), copyright © James Berry 1988, reprinted by permission of The Peters Fraser & Dunlop Group Ltd on behalf of James Berry and of Harcourt, Inc. RICHARD CALEY: 'Blue is

Cover Illustrations by Chris Smedley
Inside Illustrations by

Matt Buckingham   Chris Mould   Chris Smedley

Megaleague 3000

Earth has not anything to show more fair—
the referee computer in its sphere
floats o'er the pitch with electronic ear
and cameras that zoom in everywhere
to judge on instant replay; and besides,
there are no human players any more—
their massive transfer fees made the sponsors
turn to androids whose moulded plastic hides
are easily replaced. The act's the same,
they're programmed to gesture wildly, to shout,
cry, and groan—all the rituals held dear
by the few billion who still watch the game
on real-size viddy-screens (no one goes out)
and press their buttons to boo, laugh, or cheer.

Dave Calder

Answers to Club Call:

Arsenal
Aston Villa
Derby County
Wimbledon
Carlisle United
Swindon Town
Fulham
Liverpool
Sunderland
Tottenham Hotspur
Manchester United
Nottingham Forest
Crewe Alexandra
Portsmouth
Everton
Port Vale
West Bromwich Albion
Newcastle United
Ipswich Town